MY JOURNEY INTO THE AFTERLIFE TO FIND MY SON

By Carol Lorusso

Copyright © 2025 Carol Lorusso

All rights reserved.

No part of this book may be reproduced, stored in a retrieval system, or transmitted, in any form or by any means, electronic, mechanical, photocopying, recording, or otherwise, without prior written permission from the publisher, except for brief quotations embodied in critical reviews and certain other noncommercial uses permitted by copyright law.

ISBN: 978-1-80623-584-1 (Paperback)
ISBN: 978-1-80623-585-8 (Hardback)

Printed in the United States of America

Dedication

For my son. From the time I conceived him until the time he passed on, his presence in my life taught me how to love with a love so strong, I would have given my life for him.

For my mom and dad. They took me in as a foster child when I was five weeks old. When I was two-and-a-half, there was a state law that a foster child had to be moved after this length of time to another foster home. My parents wouldn't hear of this. They had the senator in our town, the chief of police, our parish priest, among many others, sign a petition so they could legally adopt me. It worked. They legally adopted me, and I was theirs for good. I believe I was born under a lucky star because of this.

For my sister. She was thrilled that the family adopted me. My mom had given birth to her thirteen years before, and she became my second mother, older sister, and best friend.

For Mary, the mother of God. She has sent me beautiful signs since my son died. I am forever joined to her through a mother's love, for she watched her beautiful son, Jesus, be murdered in the cruelest way to save us all. What better love than this?

For everyone who has loved someone so deeply, who has passed on, that they feel they will never fill the hole in their heart—may you find hope in my story. They have not left you. They are only a veil away in the Afterlife. What was, still is.

Acknowledgments

To my husband of fifty-four years, who has supported me in the writing of this book from the very beginning. Only he loved and knew our son as much as I did. His input in this book has been invaluable to me. He has written a wonderful chapter for this book.

For the writer's group, I started in Florida, WOOF (Writers of Ocala Forum). They gave me valuable opinions from the very beginning in the planning of this book. Also, for the members of all the other writers' groups I had the good fortune to belong to, both in Florida and Massachusetts.

For my loving family and friends who are with me on earth as I write this. I am fortunate to have you in my life. You are seen. You are listened to. You are loved. I cherish the memories and laughter we share together.

Corinthians 3: *"Of these three: Faith, Hope and Love, the greatest is Love."* Jeremiah 29:11: *"For I know the plans I have for you, plans to prosper you and not to harm you, plans to give you hope and a future."*

"Mommy, people love me, and I love people too." — Adam, at four years old

Prologue

I am no stranger to loss. I am no stranger to love. Do you have a price to pay for loving someone with all your heart? Of course.

When they pass on, you long to still be able to love them, to hug them, and hold them near. When my son passed on, I tried so many things—travel, retail therapy, adventures. None of them worked. After trying all of these with no success, I had to find a way to heal my broken wing and find a Band-Aid for the hole in my heart. What finally worked was to enhance my frequency so my soul on earth could meet his soul in Heaven through a window to the Afterlife. It has been the most wonderful journey of my life. Because of this, I am able to laugh and dance to my own life's song again, knowing my son, Adam, has never left me. We communicate all the time—through the lights in our home and sometimes wherever I visit, through dreams, through winged creatures, through electronic devices, through music, through events, and the list goes on. He is only a veil away.

In this book, I will tell you about the numerous signs I've received and continue to receive every week from my loved ones who have transitioned. I will also teach you everything you can do to make yourself receptive to meeting your loved ones across the veil, where they watch over you from Heaven. May you find hope in the following pages. May you hear the sound of your own laughter, and may you find joy and dance like nobody's watching.

Let's begin our journey together.

Contents

1. His Bright Light 1
2. On Eagle's Wings 4
3. Signs from Mary, Queen of the Angels 8
4. Dreams of My Loved Ones in Heaven 12
5. How to Become Receptive to Receiving Signs from the Afterlife 20
6. Communication Through the Lights and Other Electronic Devices 23
7. Communication Through Music 26
8. Signs From God's Winged Creatures 28
9. Testimonies From Others 32
10. Dad Brought Mom Back to Say Goodbye 36
11. The Double Rainbow 38
12. Forgiveness in the Afterlife 41
13. Visitations 44
14. Attending a Consoling Event 51
15. My Most Memorable Vacation 55
16. Adam's Illness and Passing 58
17. My Depression and Surviving COVID and Double Pneumonia 67
18. Reflections on Memories 72
    Epilogue 83
    About the Author 84

CHAPTER 1

His Bright Light

Adam was the center of his basketball team. We were fortunate to see Adam get 20 out of 20 baskets from the foul line, even after he became ill. During a game at his school, he won the game for his team when they were behind, scoring three points from across the court right before the buzzer went off to end the game. His teammates carried him off the court on their shoulders in celebration. What a wonderful evening that was!

Adam played soccer until he was picked for his basketball team. We knew it was time for him to concentrate on basketball when he carried his basketball to soccer practice.

Adam was amazed to see Danny Ainge of the Celtics get 20 out of 20 baskets from the foul line when we sent him to Danny's basketball camp. Later, Adam did the same. He could also slam-dunk. His friends told us that Adam never bragged about the fact that he was the only one in his circle of friends who could do this. For him, it was all about teamwork. Adam stood six feet three inches tall and weighed 205 pounds. He was muscular, with a frame like a basketball player—strong, with warm, dark brown eyes and brown hair. He always greeted everyone he met with a warm handshake and a "hello," and a joyful, sincere smile.

Three years after Adam passed on, we were on a ghost tour on Father's Day, as they had a special where fathers were admitted free. The woman leading the tour didn't tell us she was an evidential medium and psychic, but my husband and I would soon find out. When we were outside a mansion with twenty others who were on the tour, our tour leader and some of the others began talking about orbs. Our leader kept looking around my face with a serene smile. I asked, "Why do you keep looking around me and smiling? Do you like my hat?" She replied, "You have a beautiful angel surrounding you. His light is so bright that when I look at you, I'm blinded. I hear the dribble of a basketball coming from him. He loves you very much." Imagine our reaction! Pure evidence that what a soul loves on earth follows him into the Afterlife.

Adam had lived his 35 years on earth without guile. If a friend treated him badly during one of their excursions, he always defended that friend, saying, "His life isn't as happy as mine. He doesn't mean it if he's critical or grouchy. He's just been through a hard time. I can't be angry at him." Adam also never met a stranger. He could hold a conversation with the oldest and the youngest. I remember the day he taught one of our friends' little boys to play the bongos at the beach. From the time Adam was small, I told him to always make others feel special, and to enter a room with the attitude, *"Look at you, you're special,"* never entering a room with the attitude, *"Look at me."*

My husband had a close friend named Mike, who passed away at 42 from melanoma. When Mike called our home, he was always happy when Adam answered the phone because he made Mike feel special. The librarians Adam chatted with while we attended our writers' group said his warm smile and *joie de vivre* always made their day. The lab technicians who drew his blood loved hearing Adam's joyful account of everything the three of us had done over the weekend—like swimming in the Gulf at sunset and joining a drum circle on the beach.

He loved to race his model cars, and my husband helped him in the building of all of them. Adam had a close friend who would travel two hours so they could race their radio control cars together at a place where people raced these cars. My husband and I loved being in the audience watching, and we often took Adam to the hobby stores to buy things for his cars. Music was also a big love of his, and he loved playing his electronic drums. Movies were another love. An older man at a movie and bookstore we frequented thought Adam was a savant because Adam knew the names of all the actors, directors, and producers of movies he enjoyed. The man who owned the hobby store Adam frequented thought the same.

So you see, a soul does not shed their personality or what they enjoyed most on earth in the Afterlife. It remains the same. On that Father's Day, the evidence the medium gave us was astounding—and she only knew us as Carol and Paul, who were on the tour she led.

CHAPTER 2

On Eagle's Wings

The souls of our loved ones are able to reach out to us through winged messengers on earth. Throughout this book, I will give you many examples of this.

When Adam became ill with schizophrenia in 1991, it was a long, hard road to travel. He was hospitalized for the first time for eight weeks in a young person's psychiatric hospital so that he wouldn't experience anything that might scare him there, because he was 15. Some of the older young patients there watched over him, along with the caring younger staff. Adam became the ping-pong champion there, for he brought his same eye-hand coordination to that game that he brought to basketball.

The staff was wonderful and got to know my husband and me very well. They even knew my favorite movie was *Somewhere in Time*, starring Christopher Reeve and Jane Seymour, with the mesmerizing musical score by the great John Barry.

Our parish priest and pastor visited him once a week and left us a heartfelt letter about the visit. My husband and I went every day, coordinating our visits with our jobs, which were an hour away. Only once did I visit without my husband, as he had tactical team practice that evening. That night was a brisk, extremely cold night in Massachusetts. I remember raising my arms up to the half-moon and stars that evening, praying to God alone in the parking lot to heal my son, and thinking, *"This indeed is what it feels like—alone in the dark, hoping for a miracle."*

The miracle came the next time Adam was admitted in the spring of 1992, when he was put on Clozapine, which was known as the "miracle medication for schizophrenia" at that time. It brought our son back, but he passed on 17 years later from a bowel obstruction and sepsis, and could not fight this as his white blood count was too low. It had dropped from a normal 8.2 to 1.7 within 16 days after Adam had his blood drawn. The protocol is to be able to receive his medication every month to monitor his white blood count on this medication. He initially had to have his blood drawn once a week to monitor his blood levels on this medication. Then the Federal Drug Administration changed the visits to the lab for schizophrenic patients to every two weeks and then to once a month, so Adam became collateral damage because of this new protocol. Our brightest light in our lives would leave us to be with Jesus.

During those years after his diagnosis until his passing, Adam went to a special high school for one year and then went back to his regular high school. Everyone applauded Adam and another boy who had been in a skiing accident at his graduation. Adam waved his diploma in the air with a big smile when he received it. It was wonderful—a long-awaited evening in his high school gym, filled to capacity. Adam later graduated from community college with honors, earning a certificate in business.

When he started working, Adam preferred working with animals and plants, for he always had a love for animals and being around them and caring for them, and plants brought him solace and enjoyment. At the lion and tiger sanctuary in our town, where Adam volunteered, they named a bear cub after him, for a female bear took a liking to him and stretched her arms out whenever she saw him. He enjoyed feeding the bears, the company of all the others who worked there, and making the young girls laugh who also volunteered there. He loved the owners in charge and would be up and ready with his lunch made to go there. I never had to wake him up to get ready. Volunteering there brought him joy, and he loved the companionship.

During those years after Adam's diagnosis, whenever the hymn *"On Eagle's Wings"* was sung at our church, I would take his hand and whisper to him, *"You're going to soar like an eagle."* One day, two years after Adam had passed, my husband and I were getting ready to walk our dogs at Cross Creek, the state park where the writer Marjorie Rawlings wrote the famous Pulitzer Prize-winning book *The Yearling,* and other novels and cookbooks. Before we left that morning, I asked, *"Adam, it has been a while since I've received a sign from a bird. Could you please send me one?"*

As we drove 20 minutes away to Cross Creek, a beautiful, huge American bald eagle with a white head and white tail flew a few feet directly across from our windshield! It paused, looked me directly in the eyes with its golden eyes, then, turning with its left wing up to the sky and its right wing by its side, soared up to the sky! My husband and I looked at each other in disbelief—I had received my sign!

"On Eagle's Wings" — *chorus*

"And He will raise you up on eagle's wings, bear you on the breath of dawn, make you to shine like the sun, and hold you in the palm of His hand."

My husband and I sing in our church choir. Every time we sing this hymn, I have to stop myself from crying tears of joy, remembering that day.

Eagles have a regal aura and profound capacity to traverse the window between Heaven and Earth. An eagle represents loyalty and serves as a guardian in the winged kingdom with its celestial ascent, bringing solace that our departed loved ones watch over us from Heaven.

CHAPTER 3

Signs from Mary, Queen of the Angels

The Blessed Virgin has appeared to me in many ways to comfort me after Adam's passing. We had attended a family wedding in Massachusetts and were headed on our road trip back home. During the wedding reception, there was a dance where the women danced with their sons. I held back my tears. Whenever we were with family and friends, if everyone else was too tired to dance, Adam knew how much I loved to dance, and he would dance with me. I taught Adam how to dance from the time he was a little boy, and he was a natural at it. My husband used to tease us and say that when he saw us dancing in our living room, it reminded him of Jenny teaching Forrest to dance in a scene from *Forrest Gump*. I got through that dance at the wedding by telling our Aunt Nora how I felt and conversing with her.

As we headed home, we stopped in a clothing store in Virginia. It sold only clothing, but there was one magnetic sign for sale on the wall. It was of the Blessed Mother wearing a jeweled crown. The writing on the sign said, *"Hope will find you."* I purchased that sign, knowing it was meant for me. It hangs in our dining room to this very day.

My friend and gifted psychic, Aurora Collins, told me during a reading that Adam would be sending me a bouquet of roses, but it would not be a bouquet delivery that would arrive at our home. She said when I saw it, I would know it was there for me. We were at Bike Week in Daytona when I saw it. There, amongst the sweatshirts with pictures of Marilyn Monroe and skeleton heads, was a beautiful picture of Mary on a pink sweatshirt. Mary was saying her rosary, surrounded by red roses, a beautiful silver cross, and light blue angel wings. My husband and I went into the store to see if they had any others or if they had one pictured in their book. They couldn't find any. We bought the sweatshirt, and I wear it sparingly, as I want it to stay the same as the day we bought it, for the bouquet surrounding Mary was the bouquet Aurora told me Adam was sending me. This I know for sure.

My mother-in-law had passed when I had another visit with Aurora. During that reading, Aurora told me my mother-in-law was taking classes in Heaven, and she loved the Blessed Virgin very much. Aurora said my husband, Paul, and I would be standing in front of a life-size statue of Mary very soon, and Mary would be holding a single rose, which made my mother-in-law very happy in Heaven. A few weeks later, we were having a Mass for my mother-in-law at our church. The Knights of Columbus chose that Sunday to bring in and place on the altar the life-size statue of Mary as Our Lady of Guadalupe, holding the big silver rose of the Knights of Columbus. My husband and I stared at it in disbelief! As we prayed in front of it, tears streamed down our faces.

I belonged to the Legion of Mary for several years. When a legion member says their promise while holding the staff of the Blessed Virgin, many often cry because it is a sign of deep emotional connection and devotion to the Holy Spirit, who animates the Legion. In the morning, I said my promise, and many of my friends were in the church hall. A kind, older priest who would visit our parish sometimes officiated. I dressed in sky blue and white and wondered if this would happen to me. As soon as I placed my hand on the staff and started saying my promise, something so beautiful passed through me that it made me sob in complete abandonment. It was such a powerful feeling of love that simply doesn't exist in this realm. I finished my promise, sobbing the entire time.

There is no doubt in my mind that the love which emanates from the Blessed Virgin and the Holy Spirit, when it fills your soul, is something so powerful that it would bring even a non-believer to his knees. This emotional response from Legion members signifies dedication and intention to live out their promise with faith and love... a love so powerful from Heaven it encapsulates your entire soul.

Another time the Blessed Virgin sent a powerful sign to me was when I had just visited the National Shrine of Our Lady of La Leche in St. Augustine. It is an honor to be recognized as the United States' most peaceful tourist spot. There is a little wooden chapel where you can pray in silence and light a candle to Mary. Many prayers have been answered there. It is a place of complete solitude and peace. Mass is also offered daily in the church there, and off to the right as you enter the church, there is a room with a life-like statue of Our Lady of Fatima, where she appeared to the three children of Fatima multiple times, telling them prophecies. There are black-and-white pictures in that room of the people who stared with amazement as what seemed like a ball of fire descended from the sky. During the apparition in Fatima in 1917, the children reported seeing a woman more brilliant than the sun, who asked them to pray the rosary and offer sacrifices for the conversion of sinners.

Our Lady of La Leche Shrine encompasses a church, a historic chapel, a museum gift shop, and a pilgrimage center. The grounds contain trails through a rosary garden, the 14 Stations of the Cross, the seven sorrows of Mary, and a historic cemetery. I bought a print of Jesus embracing a young man entering Heaven there. It is also on the wall of my dining room. When I came back home from that pilgrimage, I was looking through some old photos of when Paul, Adam, and I were on a trolley tour when we visited St. Augustine for the first time. In one of the pictures, Adam was turned and looking and smiling at the huge cross at Our Lady of La Leche, which is so large, it would be impossible to miss from the trolley tour.

This was clearly another sign that Adam had sent me through Mary! When the Passion of Christ is said at our church, the priest goes through the fourteen stations. When he says the thirteenth station, I cry because that is when Jesus is taken down from the cross and placed in the arms of his mother. This is very powerful for me, as my thoughts go back to when my Adam coded and passed away in the hospital surgical ICU, and my loving husband had to hold me, trembling as I cried and screamed, "That's my baby. That's my little boy."

I can only imagine the intense sorrow of the Blessed Virgin as she held her beautiful son, who had been killed in the worst way to save mankind. When a mother loses her child, she thinks back to the day he was born, to his innocent childhood when she held his hand wherever they went, to his teenage years through adulthood. Jesus passed at 33. Adam passed at 35. I am sure Mary thought of all those beautiful times she had with Jesus from the time of his birth. The 13th station is considered the most powerful and heartbreaking.

In my next chapter, I will explain how Adam and my loved ones have appeared in my dreams in different stages of their lives. In Adam's case, in my most beautiful dream I write about, we started out on the road of the Afterlife, leading into Heaven with Adam as a little boy holding my hand, and then evolving in age when he went inside the crystal gates of Heaven. The following chapter has so many beautiful dreams I've been blessed with from my loved ones in Heaven.

CHAPTER 4

Dreams of My Loved Ones in Heaven

The first dream I had of my loved ones in Heaven was of my dad. Adam was 13 months old when Dad passed on. In my dream, I walked into my parents' living room. Everything was so vivid—the sights, the sounds, all the furniture, and the family photographs adorning the walls. In the middle of the living room was my dad, smiling at Adam and lifting him up in the air.

I cried, "Daddy, I miss you. Promise me you will never leave me ever again."

When my dad turned and smiled at me, he was a bit younger and his face was illuminated with a wide smile.

He replied, "I have never left you. I will always be with you, watching over you."

When I awakened, I knew I had made a connection with my dad through a window to Heaven.

These dreams are so fluid and real—nothing like the nonsensical dreams we sometimes have.

The second dream was of my father-in-law after he passed on. In the wintertime in Massachusetts, my father-in-law often wore a navy-blue woolen stocking hat around his home. Adam had a matching hat, which he wore in winter. He was six years old when my father-in-law passed. In my dream, I was barefoot and felt the blue shag rug under my feet as I entered Adam's childhood room. There, snuggling with Adam in

Adam's bed, was my father-in-law with his woolen hat. Adam slept peacefully in his arms and was wearing his matching woolen hat. As I approached them, my father-in-law looked up at me with a broad smile. He, too, was a bit younger.

I asked him, "Dad, are you happy?"

He replied, "Go back and tell them I'm happier than I've ever been."

I was told I travel in my dreams to see them in Heaven. The words from my father-in-law were somewhat proof of this when he said, "Go back and tell them ..."

These dreams are so lucid and filled with love, I do not want to awaken from them.

My dreams of Adam have been incredibly beautiful. In one dream, Adam and I started out on the path to Heaven. We were holding hands, and we were younger. He was a little boy dressed in white, and I was a young mother. We walked hand in hand as we always did. The valley around us was a beautiful, liquid green color. Red cardinals, butterflies, dragonflies, and a beautiful assortment of colored birds flew around us. Flowers sprang up along the path. They were a brilliant assortment of colors and sparkled like Fourth of July sparklers.

As we walked, I changed into the age I was when Adam passed on—58. He changed into the young man of 35 he was when he passed. As we progressed down this beautiful path and with age in my dream, Adam was still dressed all in white. He held my arm instead of my hand. That was the way we walked together when he was a man. The beautiful winged creatures continued to swirl around us. The collage of flowers kept springing up as we walked further down the path to our destination.

At the end of the path, there loomed before us a crystal gold-and-white land, encompassed by a brilliant white light. I could feel the incredible love coming from it. Adam and I did not speak. We conversed through our thoughts.

I asked, "Is that Heaven?"

He turned and looked at me with a peaceful smile and nodded, "Yes."

Still smiling at me, he faded into the bright encompassing light and the crystal gold-and-white land. I believe the destination was the entryway to Heaven.

Adam had faded into Heaven. I could not, as I am still here on earth. I had been privileged in my dream to visit the outskirts. I still have much work to accomplish before I pass on. When I am worthy to enter God's kingdom in Heaven, Adam will be there to welcome me, followed by the rest of my loved ones. Because of this, I do not fear death, for I know a loving homecoming is waiting for me after I've finished my work here on earth. For now, I intend to keep making myself worthy.

Some days I succeed. Some days I fail. I am grateful for every day I awake to try again. That's all one can do…

"Finish each day and be done with it. You have done what you could. Some blunders and absurdities no doubt crept in; forget them as soon as you can. Tomorrow is a new day. You shall begin it serenely and with too high a spirit to be encumbered with your old nonsense." — Ralph Waldo Emerson

Another dream I had of Adam was on the first Valentine's Day after his passing. I approached Valentine's Day with sadness. I always gave Adam a special gift on Valentine's Day. I prayed for a special sign from Heaven on this day. I believe Adam answered my prayers through a mutual friend of ours, Walt. Walt was a member of our writers' group. He was the first to arrive to comfort my husband and me at the hospital after Adam had passed. On Valentine's Day, Walt sent us a beautiful musical e-card. In the card, a flock of birds flew from a tall green tree into a field of flowers and rose up again as butterflies. The butterflies flew up to a bright, azure sky, which turned dark with bright, twinkling stars and a full moon. I played the card over and over again for hours. In my heart, I knew Adam had sent us this Valentine through Walt.

Two days later, I had my answer. In a dream, my husband and I walked past a conference room window leading to our writers' group. Adam sat there alone with Walt. He smiled, waved, and nodded "yes" to us. As we rounded the corner and entered the room, Adam waved again, and his image faded, leaving Walt sitting there alone. My heart soared! Our loving son had not forgotten us on Valentine's Day.

One night, I listened to a radio program during the night where the first speaker spoke of different wars. The second speaker on the radio program was a psychic. She spoke of how angels contact us. I fell into a deep sleep as I listened to this program. I had a dream that an army of beautiful, tall angels marched in formation. They were headed to stop a war.

In my sleep, I screamed, "Beautiful angels, please don't go to war. There has to be another way to save mankind!"

Adam then appeared in the dream. He was dressed in white and smiling. He held up a white banner with beautiful black lettering on it. The inscription on the banner read, "LOVE CONQUERS ALL."

My first dream of Adam occurred the first night he passed on. When Adam was little, I made up songs with his name in them. One of them was "What's the matter with Adam? He's alright. What's the matter with Adam? He's okay."

One of Adam's first words as he sat in his little red rocking chair was, "He's *alright. He's okay.*"

The night of his passing, in my dream, Adam opened his bedroom door and walked down the hallway towards me. He said, "Mommy, I'm alright. I'm okay."

My second beagle passed from tracheal paralysis and pneumonia. She could not breathe. My husband brought her to the animal hospital, where they swept her up in their arms and immediately intubated her. I had stayed home to shower and dress because the evening before, we had admitted her to an affiliated hospital that was closer. I didn't sleep at all. I waited for a call from them to hear if she was okay. We picked her up in the morning and brought her to our regular vet. They started an IV on her.

We picked her up from there at noon, as they closed at noon on a Saturday. We had her home only an hour before she was in distress, struggling to breathe. That's when my husband took her and told me he would come back for me. On the way to the animal hospital, he drove with one hand and held her close with the other. He wanted her to know how much she was loved. When I arrived at the hospital, they told me it would be over four thousand dollars a day to keep her alive, and they didn't think her quality of life would come back. We heard what no pet owner wants to hear.

When we signed the papers, the young female vet started the first IV. When she asked if she could start the second IV, my husband joked he had to leave the room. He tells everyone he *folded up like a card table.* He had already shown his love for her as he held her while driving to the hospital. I stayed in the room.

I spoke to Molly, "Remember when I adopted you in our city square and you were a year and a half? Our wonderful adventures we've had together began on that day." Then I kissed her face and stroked her. I sang to her when the second IV was administered. I chose to sing *Warmer Than Springtime Are You* from *South Pacific*. She appeared to be smiling and at peace. I don't know how I was able to do this without breaking down. Love guided me through, as it had guided my husband on the ride to the hospital.

The vet hugged me and said, "That was beautiful." Then we wept for a minute in each other's arms. Soon, Molly would appear to me in my dreams. In the first dream, Molly lay on our living room floor. When I spoke to her, she jumped up and ran towards me. My second dream of Molly came from my dear mother, who had passed on in 1997. In that dream, my mom wore a rustling maxi skirt with a flowered blouse. She took me by the hand and walked me to a quilt on the floor. The quilt had many colors. She lifted the quilt, and Molly jumped up from it, happy and active again! She had crossed the Rainbow Bridge and was healthy!

My dad passed away in 1975 at the age of 68. My mom passed away in 1997 at the age of 87. After she passed, I had a dream where both of them embraced me on the front porch of our family home. They led me inside the living room, where my relatives and friends who had passed on were having a party. I asked where a friend of mine was. This friend is still here on earth and very much alive. My parents had a sad look on their faces. They escorted me back through the front door to our front porch. They embraced me again and then let me go.

I had a dream of a dear childhood friend of mine who committed suicide when she was 52. She had been sexually abused by her father. She had a beautiful soul and was a nurse. She treated her patients with tenderness and love. She was prone to depression. She confided to another friend of mine and me at dinner one night that she was in touch with her counselor every day. She felt another depression coming on. The three of us had a long dinner together that evening. I was not doing that well either, for I had experienced a major depression the year before and was fighting for it not to happen again. I told her my parents would have stepped in if they knew what she was going through in our teenage years. It took a long time for her to tell my other friend and me.

That evening, the three of us talked and talked. We were as close as ever. We kept hugging at the end of the evening. Two weeks later, my other friend called. She was glad my husband answered and told him to tell me gently that our loving friend had taken her life. She simply walked into the woods and took some medication. She fell asleep in the woods—her peaceful place. Our dear friend appeared to me shortly after in a dream. We were young again and pushing our children in their strollers. She was dressed in jeans and a white shirt. She was beautiful, with the long waist-length hair she had when she was younger. We were headed to our other friend's home.

I asked, "Are you happy?"

She nodded with a sweet smile. "Oh yes, I finally got it right this time."

This I know for sure—many who take their own lives are ill at the time with depression. Sensitive souls often fall into depression, for they love others without any reservations, often forgetting about themselves. Yes, our merciful and loving God embraces them in the love of Heaven's light.

They are no longer in pain. Many of them hide their pain from others and are people pleasers who do not want to burden others when they fall into that dark well of depression. My girlfriend had a beautiful, loving soul on earth, and she continues on in Heaven with that same gentle soul.

Before I go into the next many chapters where I explain how I am contacted in many ways from my loved ones in Heaven, my next chapter will give many suggestions on how you can become receptive to receiving these signs. Remember, we are on this journey together, and what was, still is.

CHAPTER 5

How to Become Receptive to Receiving Signs from the Afterlife

Do not hesitate to ask your loved ones who have passed on for signs from them. Simply tell them how much you love and miss them. Tell them you are open to receiving these signs and how happy it will make you if they send them and communicate with you.

When you begin your day, go to a place of solitude and peace and meditate. We all have our own way of meditating. I sit in our yard and listen to the sounds of nature. I listen to the birds singing, notice the flowers blooming, and the way a gentle breeze passes through and rustles the leaves on the trees. Then, I begin talking to God the Creator, Jesus, Mary, the Holy Spirit, Archangels Michael, Gabriel, Raphael, and Uriel, Saint Francis, and Saint Joseph. I talk to Adam, my mom and dad, my sister and brother-in-law, my Godchild, in-laws, relatives, and friends who have passed on. I tell them how much I love them and think of the beautiful memories I have of them. I spend about ten minutes in this softly whispered conversation. Then I recite the Our Father and the Hail Mary. I then end by reciting the five Reiki principles to begin my day in a serene way.

It is important to be mindful as you go about your day. Notice the winged creatures around you. Try to spend time in nature every day. I could have missed so many signs from God's winged creatures if I weren't mindful and present. Notice the signs on billboards and businesses when you drive. Many of them will contain a word or sign coming from

Heaven. For example, my dear friend, who was the owner of the animal sanctuary where Adam worked, passed on. After we went to her funeral and celebration of life, I asked Adam to send me a sign letting me know they had met in Heaven. My husband and I were driving along a busy route in the city, a few hours later. My friend's last name was Bowen. I noticed the names of two businesses which were near each other—Bowen Glass and Adam's Electrical! My mother would often say, "I'm all in" when she was tired. I noticed a sign of a business near us called *The All Inn*.

Notice the sunrise, rainbows, sunsets, moon, and stars. When I'm outside, I hold my arms out and up to them. For me, it helps me to experience them fully.

Set your intentions for the day. Include in your intentions how you will make someone's day better by making them feel special—by complimenting them or by simply listening to them. Being a good listener is one of the greatest gifts you can give someone. If you have days where you stay home, call a friend or relative, or text them, or write a letter to them. Whatever you do, have your heart chakra lead the way. Try to be a Lightworker on Earth. Say, "I love you" *or* "I appreciate you." Let others know how their presence in your life is a blessing. Hug others often. Let them know how special and important they are.

Take examples from children and animals. They live in the present and appreciate and notice little things. Run through the sprinklers barefoot, roll down a hill, relish the taste of ice cream or a popsicle, and dance like nobody's watching.

Remove all guile, thoughts of anger or envy from your life, or memories of how someone wronged you. Tell yourself you have no room in your life for such nonsense, for you want to ascend in thought so you feel you have touched the face of God through your heartlight.

Keep a grateful journal of everything you've encountered during your day that brought you joy, and of your loved ones you shared laughter and conversation with during the day. End your day with happy memories of your loved ones. Ask them to watch over you as you sleep. The day has come to an end. Relish in your rest time. Know you did the best you could. Set good intentions for the next day and let peace envelop you.

CHAPTER 6

Communication Through the Lights and Other Electronic Devices

When Adam first passed on, the ceiling light had blown out over our kitchen table and had to be replaced. Before we replaced it, it came on brightly and blinked. This amazed me! I looked at it and asked, "Is that you, Adam?" It blinked once—"Yes."

I then said, "I love you." It replied with three blinks back. I knew I had a simultaneous frequency with Adam through that light that was supposedly burnt out. Fast forward—we communicate through that light. We have not touched it and have left it the same. It is an undeniable connection to Adam. It always begins with it blinking three times, "I love you," to which I reply the same, "I love you." When I question Adam through the light, one blink means "yes" and two blinks mean "no."

Before our Godchild, Katy, passed on in the hospital from pneumonia and the autoimmune disease vascular arteritis, I asked Adam if she would pull through. I received a much longer answer. The light blinked for a long time, blinking longer and shorter. I deciphered the message as telling me that Katy was halfway in Heaven and halfway on earth. She wanted to continue to be at peace and be free to enter Heaven. She regretted leaving everyone on earth, but she was very tired of fighting this autoimmune disease, which had her taking many medications that produced side effects. She had seen how she would be healthy again in Paradise and wanted to leave. She passed on the day after I had the conversation with Adam, through the kitchen light. Katy was free from illness and healthy again.

One evening, I asked Adam through the light what I already knew the answer to. I asked, "Adam, is Jesus the way, the truth, and the life?" What happened next amazed me! The light surrounded my entire being for about six seconds. It was such a brilliant, encapsulating light of love! I wept with joy, covering my tears with my hands.

My husband sees this correspondence between Adam and me all the time, and it never ceases to amaze him. One evening, when we were watching *Mr. Holland's Opus* and it came to the part where John Lennon's song, *Beautiful Boy*, came on, we both cried thinking of our Adam. Immediately, all the lights, television, and radio went on and off at the same time! We looked at each other in disbelief. Our Adam was letting us know he was right there with us.

My husband had hip replacement surgery three years ago. The physical therapist came three times a week for about a month to work with him. On one of her last visits, she remarked that she was happy I stayed in the living room to observe the exercises she taught him so I could learn them. At the moment she said that, all the lights and electronics went on and off several times again in the living room. Then, I happened to look down near where I was sitting on the sofa. Sitting next to me was a white feather in the shape of a small angel with wings—a cherished gift from Heaven.

I was on a weekend away with some friends. We were waiting to be brought to our table by the hostess at the restaurant. As she brought us to the larger dining area in the back, all the lights in the rooms we walked through started blinking on and off. They, too, all noticed that happening and spoke of it as we sat down.

Whenever we have a thunderstorm and we lose power for several days, my husband and I notice the light in the front of our home stays on, even though we have no electricity. We believe Adam is protecting and guarding our home.

When I walked from our car towards the supermarket one afternoon, the alarms on an entire row of cars went off as I passed them!

After my sister passed on in our home, I put on her light pink cardigan sweater to comfort me. As I did this, the radio went on by itself in our living room. Adam's picture showed up as the wallpaper on my computer. This lasted for two weeks.

On the first few Mother's Days after Adam passed, my cell phone would ring in the middle of the night. It kept ringing until I was awake enough to pick it up. The number calling in always registered as 000-000-0000!

There was a movie called *Frequency,* which dealt with this electrical phenomenon. It is a comforting communication of love from our loved ones in the Afterlife. When our frequency goes up and their frequency comes down, we meet in the middle through the window to the Afterlife.

CHAPTER 7

Communication Through Music

Adam's favorite song was the medley of *Somewhere Over the Rainbow/What a Wonderful World* by Israel IZ Kamakawiwo'ole. He loved to sing this and, during the *What a Wonderful World* part, he would make his voice sound exactly like Louis Armstrong's. Since his passing, this song is sung and played wherever I go. I'll sit down at a concert and the choir begins singing it. If I've had a bit of a hard day, I'll sit down at a restaurant or café and it begins playing. I close my eyes, and any worries I may have drift away.

We had *I'll Be Seeing You* and *Smile* played at Adam's funeral along with *On Eagle's Wings, Be Not Afraid,* and other hymns. We also had Neil Sedaka's song with the words he wrote in English, *Through the Hands of Time,* to the tune of *Nessun Dorma* played at the funeral. For quite some time after, these songs would come on when we turned on the radio and when we sat down at coffee shops and restaurants.

I taught Adam how to fast dance to many Donna Summer songs. Her songs come on often as I drive down the road to our home. The year after Adam passed, I went to Massachusetts for a week to visit friends and relatives. I had breakfast one morning at a favorite restaurant with my sister and brother-in-law. After breakfast, I whispered to Adam, "If you're here visiting with me, can you send me a sign?" We then walked into a gift shop, and *On the Radio* by Donna Summer started playing.

Adam loved music and playing his electronic drums. He was a good dancer, and I am happy I danced with him as often as I did. One evening, we were at karaoke with friends, and Adam sang and danced to *Little Red Corvette* by Prince. He was completely off-key, but that didn't matter. He was having such a good time, and the women there liked the way he looked. They started throwing their hats and scarves at him!

I always thought I would dance with Adam at his wedding to *What a Wonderful World,* but it wasn't meant to be. I am grateful for the treasured memories I have of the many times we danced together.

There's a beautiful song from the Skyliners that was a hit when I was a little girl. I play it almost every day. It reminds me of a simpler, innocent time. I can picture my sister, Rita, looking beautiful as she left in her pink strapless gown for her junior prom. As I listen to this song and sometimes dance to it with my husband, tears always gently roll down my face, remembering that carefree, magical time in my life spent with my beloved family.

I hope you listen to all the beautiful songs that bring back memories of times spent with your loved ones who have passed on. I hope you sing and dance to them with a joyful heart and feel the love.

CHAPTER 8

Signs From God's Winged Creatures

In the chapter on *Eagle's Wings*, I wrote about the beautiful sign we received from Heaven from the magnificent eagle.

In this chapter, I will tell you how different birds, butterflies, and dragonflies have appeared to me with messages from the spirit world. I experience these on a weekly basis, and I learned to be present and mindful of nature around me so I know them when they appear.

We celebrated Adam's birthday on the beach with our dear friends on his birth date of June 29th, even though he had passed the previous October 30th. I just could not let the day pass without buying a cake and singing *Happy Birthday* to him. Our friends, their daughter, my husband, and I sat around the birthday cake I had bought, singing *Happy Birthday* in unison. When we did this, a raven flew on the hood of our friend's car, looked each one of us in the eyes, and chirped loudly as if speaking to us. It did not fly to anyone else on the beach that day, not even to others who were having a picnic.

It came back fifteen minutes later and again looked at us and chirped loudly. When I had a phone conversation with a famous psychic/medium from the Midwest, she told me Adam said he had put his soul into that bird that day to join his birthday party because, when a soul passes on, it has the ability to be everywhere at once. We all looked at each other, amazed at the way the bird had joined the birthday celebration. We were happy it had and laughed. I knew at the time that Adam was letting us know he was there, celebrating with us. My phone call with the medium confirmed this—evidence that our loved ones can cross the veil of the Afterlife to be with us.

During the year after Adam's passing, white birds began to appear to us and still do to this day. One day, the traffic in St. Augustine came to a halt when we were visiting there. I stepped out of our car to see what was happening. I was stunned to see about thirty white birds that had flown across the street from the bay swirling around our car. They did not fly to any of the other cars that were stopped. Many times, we will be driving along, and what appears to be a white dove will land on our hood and then fly away. White birds fly directly in front of us during the day and also during the night, with one wing lifted towards the sky.

A year ago, after I had enjoyed sitting in our front yard for a while, I arose to arrange our lawn chairs. I looked up, and a huge brown owl came towards me with a tiny owl and flew directly at me! I didn't have time to move or be afraid as it looked directly into my eyes and skimmed the top of my head before they both flew away. My husband was climbing the stairs to our side door, saw this happening, and froze. He couldn't believe his eyes. It is a rare occurrence to see an owl during the day, never mind them flying at you and skimming the top of your head! I wasn't afraid, as I knew it was a sign from the spiritual realm.

One day, on the anniversary of Adam's passing, I wrote about him on my computer. A tiny sparrow entered our home through the side door and sat next to me, chirping. I was joyful, for I knew this was a sign Adam was there in spirit. After the short visit from the little visitor, I led it to the front door where I set it free.

I was nervous about going to the movies alone one evening when I didn't feel well enough to work with my husband and other friends at our church's fish fry, and I didn't want to spread my cold to them. So, I decided to go to the movies alone and see *Miracles From Heaven*. A white butterfly flew near my car the entire length of our road. When I exited the car to go into the theater, a white butterfly flew around me. When I returned home in the dark that evening, a white butterfly again flew the entire length of the road beside my car. My loved ones knew I had been nervous to drive alone in the dark, so they sent a winged companion to me as my escort.

When I walk into our yard in the morning, a different colored dragonfly often flies before me. The amazing thing is, whichever dragonfly crosses my path, its colors match the colors of my dress—for example, purple and rose, yellow, blue, and silver. A huge orange-and-black monarch butterfly flies around me and sometimes rests on my shoulder or hands for several seconds.

When I'm sitting in my yard, I often ask for a sign from a red cardinal. I never have to wait long for the bright red pair of cardinals to land in a tree near me, both staring at me at the same time. We have even had them pecking at our kitchen window!

Many years ago, I was looking through books at a bookstore in an indoor mall. A little bluebird landed inside near me. It stood near me, looking up at me for about five minutes before it flew away.

Just last week, as we drove down our road, a huge, beautiful hawk flew out of the bushes and circled around our car before it flew away.

Ravens are viewed as spiritual messengers that represent inner healing and personal transformation.

Seeing an owl during the day is a lucky sign. An encounter with an owl brings information about your connection to your intuition and inner knowledge, intertwined with your spiritual life.

Seeing white birds symbolizes purity, hope, new beginnings, and divine guidance. They serve as spiritual messengers from the higher realms. White birds bring a spiritual connection between Heaven and earth—a relationship between people and God. White doves represent the presence of the Holy Spirit. Encounters with white birds, especially white doves, are equated with gentleness, kindness, and love.

White butterflies signify love and guidance from the spiritual realm.

All butterflies signify a powerful spiritual sign of transformation.

The spiritual meaning of dragonflies is transformation, change, and new beginnings.

Sparrows are associated with divine protection, joy, and resilience.

Bluebirds signify joy, hope, and renewal.

Hawks symbolize spiritual guidance, wisdom, and vision.

Seeing two red cardinals symbolizes a connection to those who have passed. They bring you a sign from the spiritual realm, letting you know your loved ones are watching over you from Heaven, offering comfort and guidance.

CHAPTER 9

Testimonies From Others

My husband, Paul, has experienced the lights going on and off and other electronic devices doing the same in our home, and it never ceases to amaze him. Red cardinals always appear to him in pairs while he's working in our yard. He has been a witness to the eagle, the owls, the white birds, and the hawk. He finds coins, especially dimes, wherever he goes, as I do. His love for our Adam was selfless, and I know Adam is right beside Paul, helping him as he works on our cars, home, and yard. Paul always helped Adam in the fixing of his radio control cars. He was also a terrific drummer and showed our Adam how to play.

Our niece and Godchild, Katy, had an amazing experience. While visiting her grandma, Paul's mother, she saw a clear image of Adam dressed in a long white gown. Adam looked the same—his hair worn shorter in the front and longer in the back. He had on his wire-rim glasses. The only difference is that he was even taller than his earthly height. What amazed us when she sent us the picture via email was that Adam was walking our first Molly beagle with a leash. He did not know Molly on earth, as he had passed on before we adopted her from a shelter. When we visited with Katy in Massachusetts, the picture she took of them was as clear as an X-ray on her phone, and it even showed Molly's freckles! She told us Adam's spirit passed through her that day, and it was an experience far more beautiful than anything on earth because of the heavenly love she felt. Adam truly loved all his cousins, and I know he wanted to let Katy know he wanted to do all he could to help take away the pain of her autoimmune disease.

Our niece and nephews and Adam's cousins, Nitya and John, were very often with Adam when they were growing up. Nitya and John are my sister's children. Adam is with my sister in Heaven, and we have become Nitya's and John's "surrogate parents" on earth—a role we are happy to take on with humility and love. Nitya is a teacher of past life regression. She is a Reiki master and, with help from the heavenly realm, performs Reiki healing. She also teaches sound shamanic healing, breathwork, and yoga. She told me one day she called upon an angel to lift her up to the Seventh Dimension. She said Adam appeared, put his strong arms around her as these beautiful wings appeared in her vision, and together, they flew up to this higher realm. When you are in Nitya's presence, her personality is so full of love and joy, you know her heart chakra leads her through her work here on earth. In her first encounter from the Afterlife with Adam, who goes by Adama in Heaven, she asked him, "How are you? How are you doing?" He replied, "I came to earth as a Lightworker. In the Afterlife, I teach children and animals spirituality."

My friend, Aurora, told me that when I had my first reading with her, there was a young man whose spirit was incredibly thick around me. He is a teacher of children aged eight to fifteen who have passed away suddenly and find themselves in Heaven. They arrive a bit confused, and he makes their transition easier with his joy and sense of humor. She told me he goes by the name Adama in Heaven. This literally floored me because when Adam was little, my brother-in-law told him, "I'm going to call you Adama." Later on, when Adam was primping in the bathroom to go to a dance or club with his friends, I would hear him say, "Looking good, Adama," as I walked by.

Our friends, Elaine and Bobby, and their daughter, Gina, were with us on the beach when the raven appeared. Gina told me Adam was like a big brother to her. They often talked about the music and songs they enjoyed. When Gina went on vacation with a girlfriend and her parents to Mexico, Gina felt a bit anxious to be going to a foreign country. She said all through her vacation, she felt Adam's calming presence around her. Everywhere she went, songs they enjoyed together started playing. I know Adam was watching over her and wanted her to have a wonderful time. Gina had saved some money for incidentals for her first year of college. Instead of buying them, she bought a brick from the shrine of bricks surrounding a life-like statue of Our Lady at our church in Massachusetts, where church members have them inscribed with inscriptions to honor friends, relatives, and loved ones who have passed. We were lucky enough to see the inscribed brick and kneel before this shrine to Our Lady on a visit to Massachusetts.

Gina's older sister, Alison, had been instrumental in welcoming Adam back to his regular high school after he took a year hiatus to attend another special school when he became ill. Alison and her friends enjoyed Adam's true depiction of movie characters and their dialogue in movies they all enjoyed. One of Alison's friends had a catchy laugh—the type of laugh that makes people happy when they hear it. She sat with Adam in the study hall, and he shared his imitations with her. On occasion, this earned the two of them a detention. I know Adam appreciated that Alison helped to make his transition back to his regular high school fun. He viewed her also as a special friend and would never have let any harm come to her.

After Adam had passed, Alison was a counselor at the junior high school when a fight broke out between some of the junior high boys on the basketball court. Alison had recess duty that day and broke up that fight even though she was seven months pregnant at the time. Soon after,

Alison was leaving school at the end of the day with another teacher. She froze in the doorway of the school. Her friend asked what the matter was. She told her friend that her friend Adam, who had passed, walked past them and was the UPS man! Her friend replied that the man was the same UPS man who always delivered packages at the school. I have no doubt Adam appeared to Alison as the UPS man that day to let her know he had protected her when she broke up that fight during recess earlier in the week.

Alison also had a dream that she and a friend saw Adam called them to come down a corridor, which was lit by a bright, white light. The friend hesitated, but Alison assured her there was nothing to fear, as it was their friend Adam calling them. At the end of the corridor, they followed the bright light where Adam sat at a desk in a brightly lit room, writing. He smiled at them as they entered, and then Alison woke up.

The above testimonies are evidence that our departed loved ones appear to those they cared for on earth when they are needed the most. How wonderful that they are able to cross the veil between Heaven and earth to protect and offer comfort to their loved ones. Evidence that love of family and friends does not die. What was, still is.

CHAPTER 10

Dad Brought Mom Back to Say Goodbye

My dad passed on August 1st, 1975. My mom passed on August 2nd, 1997. Dad was 68 and Mom was 87. I could not bring myself to let her go without telling her one more time how much I loved her. She hadn't known us or my sister's family for weeks because of the small strokes to her brain she experienced. I prayed to my dad and God all day that Saturday for Mom to know us when we visited.

As we entered her hospital room, we were surprised to see her sitting up. She smiled at us, and my husband was amazed when she asked if he had enough light to read his newspaper. She greeted the three of us with a warm hug.

I told her, "You are the best mother a girl could ever want. I love you."

She responded, "I've been lucky to have two wonderful daughters, when I think of some of the problems happening in some families today."

It was a visit filled with love and memories. I thanked God and Dad in a whispered prayer on our drive home.

I called my sister, Rita, and told her, "Mom's back. She's going to be okay. I can't wait until you visit her tonight to see for yourself."

Rita called me later that evening after she and my brother-in-law came home from visiting our mom.

Rita told me, "I have no doubt what you told me about Mom coming back and holding a clear conversation with the three of you is true. I just don't understand how it happened."

My sister and brother-in-law found our mom not recognizing them or being able to speak when they visited, as we did in our future visits. My prayers had been answered during that one visit, so I could say goodbye.

What happened that day was explained to me by a man who held an event I attended a while later. He said it was as if my request and love for my mom had me climbing stairs, where my dad lowered his frequency from Heaven to meet me. The love we both felt for Mom caused her to come back through a window—a true miracle.

My husband will tell you how amazed he was when he observed this!

CHAPTER 11

The Double Rainbow

We rescued our first beagle, Molly One, from a shelter. She appeared to be much younger than her six years. She had had a litter of puppies and was abandoned in the forest by the hunters who owned her after she gave birth. She put her head on my shoulder as I held her in my arms when we drove home. She was greeted by the blue heeler who lived next door to us at the time. We later adopted the blue heeler as our own.

We owned our last Afghan hound, Myles, at the time. We had belonged to Afghan Hound Rescue of New England and had adopted five Afghans, always owning only two at a time. Myles was the last and youngest Afghan we adopted before he, too, passed on of natural causes. He and Molly were a good match and got along well together. After he passed, we had only Molly for quite a few years before we adopted our black lab/shepherd, April.

When she was the solo dog, Molly went everywhere with us. She was very adaptable and loving, and we had her for five wonderful years. She came to us positive for Lyme's. During that time, I fell in love with the beagle personality. At present, we have Molly Three, whom we adopted two months after she was born.

When Molly One passed on, I prayed to Adam, "Please send me another Molly beagle to love so I can send Molly's spirit free to cross over the Rainbow Bridge." Two days later, I saw an ad that a young beagle named Molly was being sold near us for $200. Later that week, we met and adopted Molly Two, whom I wrote about in an earlier chapter. I continued my *love affair* with beagles.

On our first outing with Molly Two, the weekend after we adopted her, we brought her to two concerts. At one concert, a little girl danced with her. We also went to a vintage motorcycle show in St. Augustine and a concert on the ocean in Daytona Beach. The Sunday evening after we had arrived home from our weekend, my husband came running in, shouting, "Carol, come quick. There's a double rainbow in the sky!"

I knew the double rainbow was a sign from Heaven that God and Adam had sent me another precious beagle to love on earth, and now, Molly One was free to cross over the Rainbow Bridge. Molly One is the beagle who appeared in Katy's photograph as she was being walked by Adam in Heaven—what amazed me is they had not met on earth.

I used to feel a dog jump on my bed in the evening at times. I would get up to check on our three, and they were fast asleep in their doggie beds. During a reading from Aurora, she told me Molly One missed me and asked Adam to put her on my bed across the veil to the Afterlife. It was her I felt!

Adam also stated that when she passed, I didn't just softly ask for another Molly beagle but pleaded for one in a loud prayer. From Heaven, my son still knows me well.

We had a German shepherd named Sarah for close to eleven years, from the time we picked her out as a new puppy. We chose her from her litter because when she saw me, she put her paws out straight, stared at me, and froze. We embarked on close to eleven wonderful years together. Before she passed on from cancer, she only managed to stand when I kissed her.

I missed two menstrual periods after she passed. When I went to work, eight pet sympathy cards lay on my desk. Sarah has come through when we attended an event by a famous, young, very gifted Catholic psychic. When he pulled us out of the crowd, he mentioned her spirit was running around our Adam's spirit in Heaven, wagging her tail, letting us know she is cancer-free.

Every time one of our Afghan hounds passed on, both my husband and I couldn't bring ourselves to put their food bowls or leashes away, for we felt their spiritual presence. Animals, like children, love with their entire being. Whether you have been away one hour, one day, or one week, they greet you at the door, tails wagging, anxious to bestow their wet kisses upon you.

I love the Karen Carpenter song, *"Bless the Beasts and the Children, for in this world, they have no voice, they have no choice. Keep them safe. Keep them warm."* The love I felt and still feel for my child and all the pets I've had and still have kept me somewhat of an eternal child. For that, I thank God—for if you become present and mindful of your surroundings, as they are experts at doing, you will know what it feels like to touch the face of our loving God, no matter what religion you practice, as long as it is ruled by LOVE.

Instead of allowing His disciples to turn away those who were bringing their infants and children to be blessed by Him, Jesus told them, "Let the children come to me and do not stop them, for it is to such as these that the Kingdom of God belongs."

CHAPTER 12

Forgiveness in the Afterlife

We had been to Massachusetts to visit our friends and relatives. During our visit, we visited a monument that was dedicated to my husband's Uncle George, which is on the corner of the street where Uncle George lived in a white three-decker home with a black wrought-iron gate and fence at its entrance. Uncle George was the neighborhood helper and Mr. Fix-it. One evening, when he was visiting his friend who owned a package store in the neighborhood before closing time, two young men walked in with guns. They demanded that Uncle George give them his wallet. When he reached into his pocket to get it, one of them shot and killed him.

After we arrived back home from our visit, I had a reading with Aurora. She mentioned Uncle George by name and described his home, the fence, and the fact that there was a monument dedicated to him on his street. She said when he crossed over into Heaven, he saw the horrible lives those two young men had lived and forgave them. This is an ultimate testimony of forgiveness from an ascended soul filled with God's bright light of love.

When a spirit in Heaven forgives someone who hurt them on earth, it signifies a profound spiritual healing and reconciliation.

Think about it—are you holding on to anger or bitterness for someone who has wronged you? My advice is—let it go. Free yourself of this earthly baggage. You do not need it in your life. It stops you from ascending into the Christ consciousness.

Forgiving someone doesn't mean reconciling with them. However, in some instances, this does happen. An example of this is if a friend or family member hurt you, took advantage of you, lied to you, etc. If you have had a good relationship with this individual and let them know your feelings, it is quite possible they didn't even know they were using you, and will not want you to end the friendship. After you have forgiven them, it often sparks a reconciliation, where the two of you decide to continue the relationship with mutual respect because it is worth saving.

If you forgive someone but do not want to continue a relationship with them, pray for them and wish them well as you both go on your separate earthly journeys. Holding on to resentment for another only hurts you, for they don't know the baggage of anger and resentment you are carrying around. Write their name on a piece of paper. On the paper, write, "I forgive you and I love you as God loves you." Afterwards, rip up the paper and throw it away. You are free from the guile that has put chains on you. Celebrate and be happy—you have washed away any resentment that was tying you down.

Forgiveness allows us to find peace and move forward. The Bible teaches us that God can forgive those who have caused us pain and encourages us to let go of anger and resentment. The act of forgiveness is seen as a divine act, where hurt is transcended, and we can rejoice in God's grace. Forgiveness in Heaven allows individuals to heal from past wrongs and find a deeper connection with their spirit. In Luke 23:34, Jesus said, *"Father, forgive them; for they know not what they do."* It reflects on Jesus' compassion and the Christian message of grace and redemption. It calls attention to Jesus' role as the Son of God and his intimate relationship with the Father.

Anne Frank wrote in her diary: *"I can shake off everything as I write; my sorrows disappear; my courage is reborn."* And also: *"In spite of everything, I still believe that people are really good at heart. I simply can't build up my hopes on a foundation consisting of confusion, misery, and death."*

I cannot read this passage without crying when I think of her writing this from age 13 to 15, while hiding with her family in Nazi-occupied Amsterdam. Her writing transforms personal reflections into a timeless testament to the human spirit.

CHAPTER 13

Visitations

Adam was attending college and didn't have to go to school that day because a snowstorm had begun. During the snowstorm, a priest and his female assistant knocked at our door to use our phone. I invited them in and served them coffee. I wondered why they had trudged up our long hill during a snowstorm when they could have gone to our neighbor's home across the street, which sat close to the road. We had a nice visit with them, and during the visit, they picked up Adam's picture and Katy's picture and smiled. When they said "goodbye," I stood at the door, and they just suddenly disappeared and left no footsteps in the snow! Was it a visitation from angels? I thought it might be at the time, but I simply do not know.

A friend I worked with told me her grandma had a visitation from St. Michael the Archangel before she passed. The family had gathered around her bed, and they heard her say, "I can go now. Michael is here and he's all dressed in white." She told me there was no one named Michael in their family, and her grandma had no friends named Michael.

My mother had an appearance from an uncle whose spirit was standing near her bed. During the visitation she had, he warned her not to marry another man she was dating besides my father at the time. Her other suitor had a drinking problem, and he warned her to end the relationship and marry my dad.

I have a visitation during the night at times when I feel a soft feather moving around my face and shoulders. Aurora told me Adam is doing this across the veil to let me know he watches over me when I sleep.

When people who are dying say they've had their loved ones from Heaven gather around them before they are about to pass on, these are called deathbed visions. These visions can include seeing deceased loved ones, angels, or even heavenly lights, which many believe provide comfort and a sense of peace as they approach death. Many individuals report experiencing these visions. They are thought to help ease the fear of death and encourage the dying to find peace, often leading to a more peaceful transition. The phenomenon is widely recognized in various cultures and religions, with many believing that these visits are signs of God's presence and support for the dying. The experience of deathbed visions is a deeply personal and often reported phenomenon, which reflects a belief in the Afterlife and the comforting role of loved ones in the heavenly realm.

My brother-in-law, Ron, had a near-death out-of-body experience in 1977 when he was involved in a nearly fatal accident. I worked on the cancer floor at the hospital at the time, when I was informed he was going to be administered the Last Rites. After he was admitted to the hospital, he felt his spirit rise above his body. He was suspended in the air, looking at his bruised body. He was at peace and felt no pain. When the doctors and nurses worked on him, his spirit joined his earthly body, and he felt intense pain and was in traction for about four months after that.

The Catholic Church has approved several notable apparitions from the Blessed Virgin Mary, including those at Lourdes, Fatima, and Guadalupe, among others.

The following is a testimony of how St. Michael the Archangel appeared to a young Marine during the Korean War. The letter has been shared in literature, read on the radio, and on television. I listen to it read late at night on the radio on Christmas night after the Christmas festivities have ended for the day. The following is the letter the soldier sent to his mom from his hospital bed after he was wounded in 1950, during the Korean War. Many internet sources say that Father Walter Muddy, Navy chaplain, was shown the letter, verified its facts, and made it public the next year at a gathering of 5,000 Marines in San Diego, California. Thereafter, the letter became famous.

The following is the text of the letter:

Dear Mom,

I wouldn't dare write this letter to anyone but you because no one else would believe it. Maybe even you will find it hard, but I have to tell somebody. First off, I am in the hospital. Now don't worry, you hear me, don't worry. I was wounded, but I am okay, you understand? Okay. The doctor says that I will be up and around in a month. But that is not what I want to tell you.

Remember when I joined the Marines last year; remember when I left, you told me to say a prayer to St. Michael every day?

"Michael, Michael of the morning, fresh crop of Heaven adorning," you know the rest of it. Well, I said it every day, sometimes when I was marching or sometimes resting. But always before I went to sleep. I even got some of the other fellows to say it.

Well, one day I was with an advanced detail way up over the front lines. We were scouting for the Commies. I was plodding in the bitter cold, my breath was like cigar smoke. I thought I knew every guy in the patrol, when alongside me came another Marine I had never met before. He was bigger than any other Marine I'd ever seen. He must have been 6'4" and built in proportion. It gave me a feeling of security to have such a body near.

Anyway, there we were trudging along. The rest of the patrol spread out.

Just to start a conversation, I said, "Cold, ain't it?" And then I laughed. Here I was with a good chance of getting killed any minute, and I am talking about the weather.

My companion seemed to understand. I heard him laugh softly.

I looked at him, "I have never seen you before. I thought I knew every man in the outfit."

"I just joined at the last minute," he replied. "The name is Michael."

"Is that so?" I said, surprised. "That is my name too."

"I know," he said and then went on, "Michael, Michael of the morning..."

I was too amazed to say anything for a minute. How did he know my name and a prayer that you had taught me? Then I smiled to myself—every guy in the outfit knew about me. Hadn't I taught the prayer to anybody who would listen? Why, now and then, they even referred to me as St. Michael.

Neither of us spoke for a time, and then he broke the silence.

"We are going to have some trouble up ahead."

He must have been in fine physical shape, or he was breathing so lightly I couldn't see his breath. Mine poured out in great clouds. There was no smile on his face now.

Trouble ahead, I thought to myself, well, with the Commies all around us, that is no great revelation. Snow began to fall in great thick globs. In a brief moment, the whole countryside was blotted out, and I was marching in a white fog of wet, sticky particles. My companion disappeared.

"Michael," I shouted in sudden alarm.

I felt his hand on my arm, his voice was rich and strong: "This will stop shortly."

It did clear up, suddenly. And then, just a short distance ahead of us, like so many dreadful realities, were seven Commies, looking rather comical in their funny hats. But there was nothing funny about them now; their guns were steady and pointed straight in our direction.

"Down, Michael!!" I yelled as I dove for cover. Even as I was hitting the ground, I looked up and saw Michael still standing, as if paralyzed by fear—or so I thought at the time. Bullets were spurting all over the place, and Mom, there was no way those Commies could have missed us at that short distance.

I jumped up to pull him down, and then I was hit. The pain was like a hot fire in my chest, and as I fell, my head swooned, and I remember thinking, "I must be dying…"

Someone was laying me down, strong arms were holding me, and laying me gently on the snow. Through the daze, I opened my eyes, and the sun seemed to blaze in my eyes. Michael was standing still, and there was a terrible splendor in his face.

Suddenly, he seemed to grow, like the sun, the splendor increasing intensely around him like the wings of an angel. As I slipped into unconsciousness, I saw that Michael held a sword in his hand, and it flashed like a million lights.

Later on, when I woke up, the rest of the guys came to see me with the sergeant.

"How did you do it, son?" he asked me.

"Where's Michael?" I asked in reply.

"Michael who?" The sergeant seemed puzzled.

"Michael, the big Marine walking with me, right up to the last moment. I saw him there as I fell."

"Son," the sergeant said gravely, "you're the only Michael in my unit. I hand-picked all you fellows, and there's only one Michael. You. And son, you weren't walking with anyone. I was watching you because you were too far off from us, and I was worried."

"Now tell me, son," he repeated, "how did you do it?"

It was the second time he had asked me that, and I found it irritating.

"How did I do what?"

"How did you kill those seven Commies? There wasn't a single bullet fired from your rifle."

"What?"

"Come on, son. They were strewn all around you, each one killed by a sword stroke."

And that, Mom, is the end of my story.

It may have been the pain, or the blazing sun, or the chilling cold—I don't know, Mom—but there is one thing I am sure about. It happened.

Love, your son,
Michael

CHAPTER 14

Attending a Consoling Event

In 2014, my husband and I attended an event at a hotel in West Palm Beach, Florida, where a young Catholic psychic/medium of 24 was holding an event with his family and would be pulling people out of the audience to give them evidence from their loved ones who had passed on. I had heard him on the radio and later saw him on television. He became so popular that he and his family were selected for their own reality show. We were both excited to attend this event and prayed that our Adam would come through.

That day, the young man divided the room of 200 people in half so he could walk down the middle aisle and get to as many people as he could. He came into the room, speaking loudly with a joyful attitude. I had loved listening to him on the radio because he was so quick and informative when he did readings for listeners who had called in. He added humor to his readings and came forth with an unbelievable amount of information and evidence as he spoke to those listeners.

He started to have every row stand up, one row at a time. The information he was giving to some of those standing was amazing. I had to visit the bathroom during his event and ran past his grandpa, who was sitting at the registration desk. I ran past his grandpa again as I returned to the room. He looked at me with a puzzled look because I was running. I wanted so badly to be back when his grandson chose our row to stand. I made it in time, for he didn't get to our row for quite some time. My husband and I were amazed as he spoke to our row.

He said to me, "You in the pink dress. You are very receptive to getting signs from Heaven, and you know they are from Heaven when you receive them. The spirits around you are driving me crazy!"

He first spoke of my dad, which literally floored me because earlier in the week, I was speaking to my dad.

I told Dad, "I miss you so much, Dad. It has been so long since we've been together on earth."

Also, earlier in the week, our wedding album flew out of our closet and hit my husband in the head. The picture of my dad handing me over to my husband at the altar fell out of our wedding album. I knew Dad was letting me know again that he is watching over me in spirit.

The young medium continued to speak to us: "Your dad is coming through, letting me know the two of you would walk and sometimes have a race in nature."

I nodded, "Yes."

He continued, "Your dad is saying it has been such a long time since I've been with my daughter in the physical form, but my spirit is watching over her all the time."

I nodded.

He then told me he saw my dad sitting at the kitchen table writing in a ledger. My dad did this every week because he was an accountant and kept his own ledger for his painting and wallpapering business.

He continued, speaking to my husband about his dad: "Your dad was very comical and performed in Vaudeville for a time."

Which was true.

"Both dads are bringing forth the spirit of a young man. I believe it is your son. He wants you both to know you did everything to save him in the hospital, and he loves you."

Then, the young man started to choke because he felt the tube they had inserted down Adam's throat after he had a respiratory arrest in the Surgical ICU.

The young medium's mother rushed to get him a glass of water, and he recovered swiftly. After the event, we were speaking to him when he signed his book that we purchased. I apologized to him, and he smiled.

"No need to apologize. Your son is a very powerful spirit in Heaven, and that's why that happened."

We were given the same evidence that my friend, Aurora, had given me about Adam, and also the medium on the ghost tour, and Kimberly from the Midwest. Our dear Adam/Adama is a teacher of children in Heaven from eight to thirteen years of age who pass on suddenly and unexpectedly, and are confused by their sudden transition into Heaven. Adam makes their transition easy with his caring and joyful teachings. Animals who have passed on surround them.

In fact, our loving German Shepherd, Sarah, came through that day also. The young medium told us her spirit was running free around our son's spirit in Heaven, wanting us to know, "I'm cancer-free. I'm cancer-free."

On that day, we left the event with happy hearts, thinking of all the evidential information the young medium had given us. We have been very lucky to cross paths with these gifted ones on earth, and to have become friends with Aurora, for they give evidence and reassurance from across the veil in Heaven. LOVE never dies. It is the saving grace we need today in this world.

The following chapter was written by my husband, Paul, in 2012 for our writers' group. It is a beautiful, treasured memory of a *golden day* we experienced with our then three-year-old son, Adam, while vacationing in the summertime in Provincetown, Cape Cod, Massachusetts.

CHAPTER 15

My Most Memorable Vacation

by Paul Lorusso

It was August 17th, 1977, the day after Elvis died. My wife, Carol, our three-year-old son, Adam, and I embarked on a trip to Provincetown from our home in Spencer, Massachusetts. Provincetown is unique and resembles no other town in the state. It's located on the outermost tip of Cape Cod, fifty miles by sea from Boston. Erosion is slowly turning this narrow strip of land into an island. Sand dunes cover the scenic landscape, punctuated by clumps of *ammophila brevilgulata*, commonly known as dune grass. The center town still resembles a three-hundred-year-old fishing village. Shops of every type draw crowds of tourists down the central street daily.

We, however, were there to take advantage of the eight miles of bicycle trails. It would be Adam's first ride. Nearly three-quarters of this town has been left in its natural state. The bicycle trails are located here on the Cape Cod National Seashore. At his young age, we wanted Adam to experience fun on a bicycle in the most beautiful of places, so we rented two bicycles from Nelson's Riding Stables, one with a child's seat on the back.

The trails began with us riding through the tranquility of the freshwater wetlands of Beech Forest. A short hill and a panoramic view opened up ahead—ocean, sky, and sand dunes—in a place where a bicycle could never be, if it were not for the six-foot-wide asphalt that lay before us. The sights, the smells of ocean air, and the sound of the pounding surf hit the senses all at once, and the thought of riding on this small piece of land with thousands of miles of ocean before you leaves you with a sense of loss, bittersweet in a way that somehow felt romantic. We rode through large culverts used as tunnels under the roads we traveled beneath. I heard many *wees* behind me as I pedaled on.

The trails took us to Race Point Beach, named for its fierce rip tides, and Herring Cove Beach with its placid waters, and back to the tranquil freshwater wetland of Beech Forest.

We were young then. We took this day for granted. We thought things would never change. There would always be days like this, and we would always be together. We didn't even take pictures. Never once did we think that Adam would pass away before us, but it happened in October of 2009. We could not foresee, at age fifteen, Adam being diagnosed with an incurable illness, as we stood by in despair for nearly nineteen years, watching all the beautiful things in a young man's life pass him by.

Now, when I think of him and all the vacations we enjoyed after that day, when we did take pictures, I am heartened because this is the day I remember most. Maybe it was the innocence of seeing all the joy in his eyes and how we all laughed, alone with my family in the most enchanting of places, showing our toddler son how much fun this world can be. Yes, we were young and innocent. That is the gift of youth and the natural course of life. As we age, learn through our mistakes, experience triumph and loss, and see the world for what it really is, we are said to have gained wisdom. Now, with a lifetime of learning, I seem to be feeling everything.

Just the day before we rode the trails in Provincetown, a man who gave his heart and soul to his fans all over the world through his music had died at the young age of 42. Elvis was gone, and with all the excitement, somehow I had forgotten. Now I think of him often, and his music will never die. Memories of Adam come to me every day. They can never be taken away, and I'm amused that in my now so-called enlightened state of mind, it takes me back to this day, when the most important decision made all week was what we were going to do for the weekend, with the deciding factor being what would be the most fun. How wonderfully irresponsible!

We all need a place, and for some time now, and for the rest of my days, time and experience have given me a most heartwarming place to go.

CHAPTER 16

Adam's Illness and Passing

Psalms 23:6: *"Surely goodness and mercy shall follow me all the days of my life: and I will dwell in the house of the Lord forever."*

Adam was ever-present from the time he was a child. He just knew what to do when he was needed. I contracted a bad case of the flu when Adam was two. My husband, Paul, a correctional officer, was forced to work a double shift at the prison that day. A snowstorm raged outside, making it impossible for my mom and dad to visit me and help me.

Adam slept near me in his white, snap-on tee shirt and pajama bottoms with our white angora kitten, Tuffy. I drifted off to sleep for a short while. When I awoke, Adam stood before me, his brown Dutch-boy-style hair covering part of his eyes. He shifted his weight from side to side.

"Mommy, I made these for you."

There, on a china plate, stood a stack of buttered toast! I hugged him and ate every last crumb. *Let the storm rage outside; there's plenty of love and warmth in here.*

When we were at a rally with hundreds of people at a retirement community, the organizers of the rally brought out bottles of water for the attendees. Adam was 32 at the time. We looked around after he left our side to see where he'd gone. He was already passing out the water to everyone!

Adam was born an empath. When he was eight, we took him to the Eastern States Exposition in Massachusetts. As we sat down under the big tent to watch the circus, we noticed a disfigured little boy sitting with his family. Adam turned to me with tears in his eyes and remarked, "Poor little guy."

At the age of fifteen, Adam became ill with schizophrenia. At first, he rationalized to us, "I suppose if anyone gets this disease, it should be me because I've had such a happy life."

One summer, my friend Elaine, Adam, and I body-surfed the waves at Daytona Beach. Elaine had a bad knee and was awaiting knee surgery. She fell in the waves and couldn't get back up. Adam lifted her until she was able to stand again.

Adam had been chosen as one of the ten super kids by the teachers when he graduated from junior high. One teacher nominated a child for the honor, and all the other teachers had to agree. This was to reward ten children who really applied themselves academically and were joyful and fun to be around, but never at anyone else's expense. We were so proud of our Adam that evening.

He entered high school and was an A and B student, and was still on the basketball team. Everything was going well until the fall of his fifteenth year. He started laughing inappropriately and seemed to be far off. He didn't confide in us at that time that he had started hearing things. His grades dropped, and his handwriting changed. It was big and not nearly as neat as it had been. I found weird drawings in his room.

We had a meeting with the school counselor, with whom I became good friends, and the school psychologist. When they informed us of the way Adam was acting in school at times, I put my face in my hands and wept at the meeting. We had always been ever-present, loving parents. My husband had been an assistant coach for Adam's soccer team and then the treasurer of the soccer association for the children in our town. I had been an assistant den mother in Cub Scouts and helped to chaperone Cub Scout outings. If I received a report that Adam was being mistreated, I handled it the very next day, like a mother lion protecting her cub.

So why, why was this happening?

When Adam left after dinner with his basketball in tow to go to the court, I would always go by in the car at the bottom of the hill, and he was always playing basketball at the court and came home afterwards.

We had an appointment to have Adam evaluated to find out what was wrong, but we found out on a cold winter's night in January. I awoke in the middle of the night to find Adam trembling and scared. I asked him what was wrong.

He replied, "Someone's outside and they're going to kill you, me, and Sarah (our dog)."

I hugged him and assured him no one was there, and I immediately called my husband at work and my sister, who lived five minutes away by car. My sister arrived with my nephew, John, within a half-hour. My husband must have sped home from work, for he worked an hour away and was home in a short time. My husband, Paul, and I left to bring Adam to the emergency room at a nearby hospital.

After what seemed like ages, a nurse called us in to speak with us. She had tears in her eyes. She told us Adam suffered from acute paranoid schizophrenia, and she gave us a small booklet on it and told us to read all the literature so we knew what was happening to our dear, sweet boy. She arranged for Adam to be admitted to a psychiatric hospital for younger people, which was an hour away. My mother-in-law, brother-in-law, and his wife arrived to support us in the waiting area while the staff admitted Adam. When we left later that night, I collapsed in tears in the elevator. *I did not want to leave my child.*

Adam was admitted to the hospital for eight weeks. Paul and I attended weekly meetings with the staff who took care of Adam. As I wrote in an earlier chapter, we visited him every day. We would take him out to the basketball court there to shoot baskets, and that's where he became a ping pong champion. We were allowed to bring him home to have dinner one evening out of the week, and then had to bring him back.

The doctors tried several antipsychotic drugs on him, but they did not *clear* him. The one that worked the best was Haldol, and he was discharged on it. It certainly wasn't perfect. It caused Adam to have tardive dyskinesia, which is a movement disorder characterized by involuntary, repetitive muscle movements, often affecting the face, tongue, and limbs. It also made him vomit up his food quite a bit.

One Sunday, after we had gone to Mass, Adam and I went to a favorite restaurant of his to have lunch afterwards. God must have been with us that day, for the dining room had emptied out by the time we finished. Adam had eaten a meatball sandwich and fries. He threw it all up after he finished eating. Before the waitress came back into the room, I ran from table to table, grabbing all the napkins and paper towels, and cleaned everything up, disposing of them in the wastebasket so she never knew. I did this to preserve my son's dignity and had succeeded, but I drove us home with a churning, upset stomach.

The second time Adam was admitted to the same hospital was in April, thirteen months later. This time, he only stayed for four weeks, and we were allowed to take him everywhere on weekends. The doctor had started Adam on Clozapine, which made headlines as the *miracle medicine* for schizophrenia. It brought our son back.

During one of our outings, we took a tour of Boston Harbor on a sailboat, and the captain allowed Adam to steer the boat.

Adam was discharged and went back to his regular high school with a warm welcome from friends and teachers. He had attended a special school for a year. One of the male counselors and Adam had a lot of good times together. They would do comical skits from *Saturday Night Live* together. I brought Adam back to visit. He wore dress pants and a dress shirt with his long, grey cashmere winter coat. The staff beamed and were so happy Adam was doing so well.

We were having his blood drawn once a week; then the FDA changed the protocol to every two weeks, then every month. We also accompanied Adam on his weekly visits to his counselor. It was very important to us that Adam retain his dignity, and his life went on happily at his old high school with many friends, and the same later at college.

There were a few times when Adam didn't take his medication on time. One time, my husband had just recovered from knee surgery, and Adam was mowing the lawn. He hadn't taken his medication on time and started slamming the lawnmower up and down. My husband ran outside, and Adam started swinging a rake at him. Adam would never have done that if he had taken his medication when he was supposed to. Even though my husband was smaller than Adam, he was able to wrestle Adam to the ground. We then brought Adam inside to take his medication. When he felt well, he apologized, and of course, the event was forgiven.

Paul and I used to have a date night every Friday night. It was the one night in the week Adam wasn't with us. I laid out his medication before we left. He enjoyed those Friday evenings, for he had pizza, watched sports on television, and listened to his favorite music on his boom box. That was also the evening he would call a close friend of his, and they would talk about their radio-controlled cars, among other things.

One night, when we returned home from our date night, I noticed Adam's eyes were very intense and that he hadn't taken his medication. He heard me say to my husband, "If he does this again, he's going to have to come with us on Friday evenings."

Adam then ran towards me, shook his fist at me, and screamed, "Do not talk about me like I'm not here."

My husband intervened and sent me to bed to rest. He finally got Adam to take his medication at 5 a.m. the next morning. *I was wrong. It was the one time being a worried mother had me take my son's dignity away.*

The next morning, as I made breakfast, Adam hugged me with his traditional two pats on the back. "I'm sorry, Mommy. I would never have hurt you. I wasn't myself. I love you very much."

I replied, "I love you so much, and there's nothing to forgive."

That was the last time Adam didn't follow through and take his medication when we were away on date night.

The days and nights flew by with the Three Musketeers—Paul, Carol, and Adam—enjoying and going through life together. Until...

On October 27, 2009, we found ourselves in a hospital emergency room to have Adam checked. He had flu-like symptoms.

Many small children were there, and Adam was pushed back, so we went home and came back the next day. This time, Adam was admitted. He had a bowel obstruction caused by his medication. The doctor took him off Clozapine, and a gastric surgeon was called in to operate. That went well, but Adam developed sepsis. As I stated earlier in the book, Clozapine had caused his white blood count to drop from a normal 8.2 to 1.7 within sixteen days of having his blood drawn, and he could not fight the sepsis.

We did not leave his side for those four days except to have a quick bite, and my husband would go home for a brief time to feed our dogs. During those four days, I slept in a recliner near Adam's bed. He was concerned I wasn't getting much sleep and wanted to talk about Christmas and whether he would be getting a new set of electronic drums for Christmas. I assured him he would. He still had his easy-going, happy-go-lucky personality at that point.

Then, on October 29th, the staff sent us out to have dinner. When we came back, everything had changed. Adam had experienced a respiratory arrest and had a tube down his throat. Adam was kicking a bit and trying to remove the tube. They had my husband hold his legs down while they administered a paralytic. Our faces were drenched with tears, and things only got worse after that. Adam lay still, but his blood pressure dropped and dropped, even though they had a machine on him to stop this.

On October 30th, they sent us out into the garden while they bathed Adam. A young couple sat out there, and the girl was crying because her grandma was going to pass on.

I remarked, "It's a beautiful October day with the sun shining. Everything will go on as usual, but our lives will never be the same. It just doesn't seem fair."

When we reentered the Surgical ICU, I heard them call a code, and we saw everyone run into our son's room. I had worked in hospitals for almost twenty-seven years and had taken part in many codes. *I wanted to jump out of my skin.* My dear husband had to hold me back as I screamed. Then, it was finished. Adam's soul left to go with God.

When I screamed, "That's my baby, that's my little boy," I noticed the male EKG technician was crying. We went in and kissed Adam with his tubes in, and then again when they took the tubes out. He looked so good—like he could have gotten up and walked out of the hospital.

The hospital psychiatrist came over to console us. She remarked, "He has a beautiful body. There isn't a mark on him. You did a wonderful job."

Guess what—I never thought our sweet Adam would pass on before us. *How do we live without you?*

The next morning, I forced myself out of bed to shower and get dressed. I knew if I didn't do it then, I probably would not be able to do it for months. We started making the funeral arrangements and finished calling everyone.

At the funeral, we were amazed by how many friends and relatives came and how many flowers there were, besides our own. The Anglican priest met with us and gave his talk about Adam afterwards. Then a friend of ours spoke about Adam, and then Paul and I gave the eulogy. Even then, the lights were blinking throughout the ceremony…

A month later, we attended our first Bereaved Parents meeting. We needed to be there, as these were the only people who truly knew how we felt. We sat and listened intently as everyone told how their child had passed on, and then we spoke of Adam. When we had pastry and coffee after, my husband felt nauseous, excused himself, and went to the car. I continued to go for a few months with a dear friend I made there without Paul. I needed to go, but it was too soon for him. He started going with me a few months later and never stopped. We cherish the friends we have made there. The signs from Adam had begun, and some of the members told us about the signs they experienced from their children.

And thus, my journey into the Afterlife began...

CHAPTER 17

My Depression and Surviving COVID and Double Pneumonia

I reached a point in my life where my spirit broke. I was warned about this by my counselor and my mom. They warned me when Adam became ill that I had forgotten all about myself and was only focused on Adam getting well. My counselor told me it wasn't good to be an oak because they break, and to be more like my husband, who was a wonderful dad, but bent and did take care of himself.

We continued to have a wonderful life with our Adam. However, in 1997, I found myself leaving work at 5 p.m., traveling to see my mother who was in her last days on earth, going home and bringing dinner or making it, doing laundry, and helping Adam with his college homework. One night, I stayed up to type his term paper, which he had written, and then went to work the next day.

In my mom's last days before she went with God, she became like a child again, screaming and crying. The day before she passed, I crawled into bed with her at hospice and sang and read to her as I stroked her hair. It was the least I could do, for she had done that for me when I was a child. I left to go have a frozen yogurt before Paul, Adam, my sister, and my brother-in-law would join me. When I came back, I noticed people who saw me were smiling—and no wonder—I had a chocolate yogurt mustache surrounding my mouth!

My mother passed on August 2nd, 1997, and my dad had passed on twenty-two years earlier, on August 1st, 1975. I wrote and gave the eulogy at my mother's Mass. After the get-together at my sister's house after the funeral, we went with Adam to meet with his counselor. During this time, our German Shepherd started having convulsions, and I would hold her and place cold water on her until they stopped. I remember holding our Shepherd, Sarah, in my arms and looking up at the sky one morning before I woke Adam to get ready for school and thinking, *I am strong. I will get through this period.*

I would get up at 5 am on a workday, walk the dogs in the dark, get ready for work, and then wake up Adam to get ready for college before we embarked on our twenty-six-mile ride into the city. My husband worked nights and was available for Adam while I was at work during the day. We managed to always have a wonderful weekend and vacation.

Then it happened. In the winter of 1998, my spirit broke. It was like a ballerina who had danced too long and broken her leg. *I could feel that darkness had come over me, and my spirit grew so tired.* Then, the day before I went on vacation, I found out the department in charge of our computer system had changed it, and I would be coming back from vacation having to put hundreds and hundreds of conferences in the computer, which my wonderful volunteer had done while I attended the continuing medical education conferences and meetings I had coordinated for the doctors. The system had been changed, and they forgot to tell our department.

After our vacation, my spirit got worse, and it broke. I sank into the deep, dark well of depression. I barely talked for six months. The only two people I allowed to visit were my sister and brother-in-law. As well as working, Paul took over traveling with Adam, tending to his needs and mine, as well as doing his household duties and mine. My husband is a very strong-minded man, but during that time, I used to watch him leave for work at night, and he looked like he had the weight of the world on his shoulders, but he never complained.

I saw a wonderful young psychiatrist who really cared about his patients.

Paul would go with me to my appointments because he knew I would try to say I was better than I was, while he told the doctor the truth—how I really was. A small number of people who go into depression have a depression as severe as the one I had.

One time, during my appointment, I remarked to the doctor, "A lot of the people in the waiting room look like they need your help more than I do." He answered, "That's why you're here, because you never think of yourself, and I'm here to take care of you and let you know you do need my help." I received wonderful care during our visits with him, and my husband and I were very grateful to him.

During that time, after Paul left for work and Adam and the dogs were sleeping, I would plan in my mind how I would kill myself and end this pain. Perhaps I would throw myself in front of a truck or train. Perhaps I would take pills, and so on. My husband even held my hand to prevent me from exiting the car when a train passed by. I did not think I would ever be the same strong, joyful, *live-and-let-live* person I had always been, but I came back. I came back because I felt the LOVE and could not leave. I will never ever let what happened to me happen again. I am a person who has journeyed to the outskirts of Heaven and found my son by raising my frequency into God's bright light of love, and I have experienced the love of the higher realm.

During my depression, I thought my friends would give up on me because they couldn't visit me. That never happened! They called constantly and brought my favorite, Greek salads, to Paul. My friend,

Susan, told me during a phone call to hug myself and repeat, "I love myself more." She even sent an adorable teddy bear with a navy blue sweater with greetings from her and my other two closest friends from work; when I pressed on it, I pressed it over and over again to hear their friendly, caring voices. Thank you, Paul, Adam, relatives, and dear friends. I love you more than you know.

In January 2021, I was admitted to Shands Hospital with COVID and double pneumonia. I thought I had the flu, but it felt very different. I lost my appetite and survived on orange juice, watermelon, water, and the occasional Greek salad for over a week. I slept constantly but became more and more ill. I struggled to breathe and knew I was experiencing COVID. Our niece and nephew sent an ambulance over to our home, but I refused to go to the hospital that evening and had Paul take me to the emergency room the next day. My friend, Kathleen, had also come over to check on us to see if we needed anything. I realize now I should have gone that evening, for I had my family in Massachusetts, Paul, and my friends here extremely worried.

I was extremely weak and could not move or hardly breathe. The next morning, I managed to shower between the coughing and wheezing spells. When we arrived in the emergency room, they put me on oxygen immediately. Little did I know I was just 3% shy of being admitted to the ICU on a ventilator. They kept me in a room in the emergency room that evening and had me eat and drink. My husband tested positive for COVID also, but they sent him home with an inhaler, as they didn't think he had to be hospitalized. He hated leaving because we both knew we would only be allowed to talk on the phone until I was discharged.

My appetite picked up after they had started multiple IVs on me. They told me I would be in the hospital for a week. I had a beautiful private room and a very special staff taking care of me. Some of the nurses took their break with me, and we watched part of a Hallmark movie or *The Golden Girls* together. I am forever thankful for the wonderful care I received. Each staff member came in with disposable outfits, which they threw away in the waste basket when they left the room. During that time, I felt my loved ones in Heaven rally around me so I would get well. I recovered a little bit earlier than they expected, and I was discharged after six days.

After my discharge, I was delighted just to go for a ride around the beautiful horse farms with my husband as we sipped our morning coffees. Having been so ill and having recovered, I was thankful just to wake up every day and enjoy the serenity of simple things and being mindful to live in the present. There is so much beauty that envelopes you when you take the time to encapsulate your mind, body, and soul in nature. My prayer for you is that you enjoy this type of serenity every day and greet each day with renewed hope.

CHAPTER 18

Reflections on Memories

Dad taught me to love rollercoasters. When I was a child, I accompanied Dad on all the rides at amusement parks, while my mom and sister played the games. I later took the tallest rollercoasters in the United States with Adam and Paul. Paul braved most of them with us, but he refused to go on the Millennium Force at Cedar Point in Ohio with us because the first dip was 305 feet high and had a beacon on top so planes wouldn't hit it. He ran around and took pictures of it as we ascended, descended, and circled at 93 miles per hour. Adam later bought a book of all the rollercoasters we had taken together.

Dad and I walked to church together on Sunday mornings when I was a young girl. After church, we always raced home, running to see who would win. I thought I was winning when, out of nowhere, my father came running using a shortcut and beat me! My friends loved my dad. When my parents had a sweet sixteen birthday party cookout for my girlfriends and me, Dad took part in all the games. My father read the Bible on his knees for twenty minutes before he went to bed every evening. At his funeral wake, a priest who accompanied one of my cousins because she worked for him told her it was the first time he attended a wake where he felt the person who had passed was a saint.

Mom was the disciplinarian in the family. My sister told me Mom wanted a doll-like little girl who would sit with company quietly and always behave. Although I did that at times, I did not listen when she told me I couldn't ride bicycles, go ice skating, or climb trees. I heard her tell a friend later in life, *"My daughter, Carol, hated confrontations. She would 'yes' me to death and then go about doing the things she wanted to do."*

I guess I never fooled Mom! She was right. I would speak in front of thousands of people without batting an eye if I were asked, but if I knew I would have a confrontation with another on any given day, I would avoid them like the plague. One day, we were having a family cookout on a beautiful summer's day. I was reading *Little Women* at the time and had just read the part where Beth died. I stayed in my room crying. My mom coaxed me out of my room by scratching at my screened window and roaring like a lion. That got me up to go join in—for how could I ignore an invitation like that?

Mom was overprotective of me because, as I mentioned before, she had had four miscarriages between the time she had my sister and adopted me. One day, I accidentally turned my bumper car around at an amusement park, where I was getting hit from all sides—but of course, you don't get hurt on bumper cars. My mom was crying in my dad's arms when she saw this. I kept trying to turn my car around for her sake, not because I was scared. *How can you get angry at your mom for loving you like that—impossible.*

I have a funny story about Mom being the disciplinarian. If I misbehaved, especially when I was home alone with her in the summer school vacation months, she would run after me with the yardstick. I would crawl underneath the kitchen table or lock myself in the bathroom until she got involved with her soap operas and forgot about the yardstick. One day, however, she did not forget. I opened the door to the bathroom, and there she was, waiting with the yardstick! I ran out the back door and through the back porch into the backyard with her running after me under the clothes that were hanging on the clothesline. An older neighbor later remarked that she had seen the funniest thing—Mom chasing me under the clothesline with the yardstick held high in her hand.

I used to tell everyone my older sister, Rita, was an angel, and I really believed she was. She dressed me up in my little red cowgirl outfit and took me to the Halloween parade in our town. I was afraid of bagpipes at the time, and I remember her wiping my tears away when they went by. I enjoy seeing and hearing bagpipes now—that fear went completely away after childhood. I remember Rita dressing me up in my yellow slicker and red boots before we headed out together on a rainy day. On one of those rainy days, we went to see the movie *Ben-Hur*. After the movie, I remember Rita holding my hand in the rain. I was crying so hard over the movie that my tears mixed in with the falling rain as they rolled down my cheeks.

Rita and I would take the bus into the city of Worcester many times on a Saturday. It was the fifties and early sixties, and everyone dressed in their Sunday best to go to the city. Rita and I wore some of our best dresses, hats, and white lace gloves. Rita wore high heels, and I wore patent leather shoes. My favorite dress was a red and white taffeta dress with little red hearts. We would have lunch at the lunch counter at Kresge's, Grant's, or Woolworth's. Lunch always consisted of a cheeseburger, fries, a Coca-Cola, and a hot fudge sundae. We then went to see a movie at one of the theaters. Before we boarded the bus home, Rita would take me shopping at Grant's in their children's department for a book or coloring book—a perfect ending to a perfect day for a little girl.

My sister passed on while vacationing in our home on October 12, 2012. She had taken ill the night before. In the morning, I kissed her goodbye before Paul and I left to buy ingredients at the market so I could make her homemade chicken soup. While we were gone, a relative from

Canada called us to get home as soon as possible. He wouldn't tell us why, so we hurried home. I had left our cell phone number on my desk, but when my brother-in-law, Ben, found my sister unresponsive, he ran to our neighbor's home for help. Our neighbor tried to revive her, but it was too late. Ben forgot our cell phone number was on my desk, but he knew Barry's number in Canada by heart, for Barry was married to his sister.

We arrived home, and I thought it was odd that only one police car was in the driveway. My husband dropped me off, and I spoke to the police officer, *"Please tell me an ambulance took my sister to the hospital, and we'll go there right away."*

The officer shook his head and said, *"She's gone."*

I was bent over, screaming, *"Please, not my Rita. Not my Rita."* My husband dropped the groceries on the ground and rushed over to comfort me.

Later on, I apologized to the officer at our home. He said, *"No need to apologize. It's actually good to enter a home where a person who has died was so loved because that's not always what we walk into."*

I closed my sister's eyes. She had passed with a smile on her face, and her eyes looked like she had seen Paradise. Aurora later told me Adam had stepped back, and my mother was the first to welcome my sister into Heaven. My *warm breeze* of a sister had gone with God. After she passed and we were back home from her funeral, where I delivered the eulogy, I used to go to our phone at times to call Rita and tell her something that had happened. I would stop short, look up, and say, *"But you already know."*

Golden memories envelop me as I age. The times spent in Newport, Rhode Island, walking the cliff walk, which overlooks the ocean and runs behind the summer mansions of what was once the summer homes of the rich, such as the Vanderbilts and the Astors. Newport, Rhode Island, had become our favorite place for Paul, Adam, and me, and we often spent the day there with friends. Days spent in Newport, Cape Cod, Maine, and Boston are forever engraved in our hearts. We always spent July 4th at the Hatshell in Boston listening to the Boston Pops and the cannon fire during the playing of the *1812 Overture*. It was followed by the largest display of fireworks over Boston Harbor that we've ever seen, and Adam loved being there with us and thousands of others every year. We sometimes brought close friends with us so they could experience the beauty of it.

I have wonderful memories of days spent with friends and relatives. Another one of my friends, named Susan, who has passed on, was present at so many events in my life. She was with me the night I met Paul at the teen nightclub when I was 18, and was a bridesmaid at my wedding. Later on, she and her husband rented from us, and our children were raised together. I have a picture of her crying after we had brought her Eric and my Adam to their first day of school. Both she and I cried, but the boys were happy to wave to us as they walked into school. We often brought our children with us to play at the park near us, where we played badminton and had picnics. We would take them to the swings overlooking the water and would push them on them and the merry-go-round. One day, they pushed us on the merry-go-round. That was a wild, memorable ride!

Paul and I would often take Adam to that park to swim. Little Adam would wrap his little legs around me and hug my neck as Paul chased us in the water, pretending to be either Jaws the fish or Jaws the guy, as Adam laughed with delight. Oh, those golden days—days filled with simple fun, enjoying being together.

I am lucky to still make memories with my Paul and my two Elaines from childhood, and my dear friend from work, Susan. In Florida, I've been lucky to acquire Kathleen as my younger *spiritual sister*, as well as many other treasured friends. My hope for you is that you make beautiful memories with loved ones, treasure them, and keep them forever tucked in your heart.

"Silently one by one,
In the infinite meadows of Heaven,
Blossomed the lovely stars,
The forget-me-nots of the angels."
—Henry Wadsworth Longfellow

Nothing Gold Can Stay

Nature's first green is gold,
Her hardest hue to hold.
Her early leaf's a flower;
But only so for an hour.
Then leaf subsides to leaf.
So Eden sank to grief,
So dawn goes down to day.
Nothing gold can stay.
—Robert Frost

Love After Love

The time will come
When, with elation,
You will greet yourself arriving
At your own door, in your own mirror,
And each will smile at the other's welcome,
And say, sit here. Eat.
You will love again the stranger that was yourself.
Give wine, give bread. Give back your heart
To itself, to the stranger who has loved you
All your life, whom you ignored
For another, who knows you by heart.
Take down the love letters from the bookshelf,
The photographs, the desperate notes,
Peel your own image from the mirror.
Sit. Feast on your life.
—Derek Walcott

Her Rescue

She wandered into the beckoning woods
Away from the highwaymen and their Tonka trunks,
Away from the cacophony of city madness.
There, she sat amongst the symphonic sounds of nature,
Her spirit in synchronicity with the wild things.
The calmness of the tall oaks soothed her,
The soft zephyrs of the wind caressed her,
The music of the birds serenaded her.
Her spirit, reborn, soaring with the assorted butterflies,
Tasting the sweet syrup of wild blueberries.
She could now return to those she loved.
With a grateful heart, she had found her rescue.
—Carol Lorusso

The Prayer of Saint Francis

Lord, make me an instrument of your peace.
Where there is hatred, let me sow love;
Where there is injury, pardon;
Where there is doubt, faith;
Where there is despair, hope;
Where there is darkness, light;
And where there is sadness, joy.

O Divine Master,
Grant that I may not seek
To be consoled as to console;
To be understood as to understand;
To be loved as to love with all my soul.

For it is in giving that we receive;
It is in pardoning that we are pardoned;
And it is in dying that we are born to eternal life.
Amen.

Epilogue

I am humbled that you have made this journey with me. Celebrate by having a glass of wine in nature while listening to the songs of the birds. Find your happy place and rejoice in the solitude. Start today to make your dreams come true. Forgive all. Listen to your loved ones. Everyone has something to say from which you can learn. Look forward without regret and be the best you can be today. Quiet your soul. *What do you want to do with your life?* If you are led by LOVE, you can never go wrong. Laugh often. Pray and meditate. Dance like nobody's watching. Write down your memories, for they are yours and yours alone. Sing and dance to your own life's song. Ascend through the Christ-consciousness, for there you will touch the face of God. And remember to *love yourself more.*

Know that there is not one true thing—as long as it is led by LOVE, kindness, and compassion, it is all true. Go to the ocean. It is eternal, as God's love for you is eternal. Run barefoot through sprinklers. Delight in the sunrise and the serenity of a new day. Relish the sunset and find peace in the twilight. Start your day praying and talking to your loved ones across the veil to the Afterlife. Talk to them in Heaven. They are with you still. Sleep as a child slumbers, as they watch over you. *You are seen. You are heard. You are LOVED.* Happy life and happy dreams, my dear friend.

About the Author

Carol Lorusso worked in the medical field for close to 27 years. She is a published columnist and poet, and a Reiki Level II practitioner. She loves to spend days at the beach with her husband, Paul. She loves to read, go to the theater, visit museums, watch old movies, and take walks on nature trails with Paul and their three dogs. She enjoys living in Florida and making memories with friends and loved ones there, as well as treasuring the memories from her life in Massachusetts. She loves to dance and swim and enjoys social events and gatherings, as well as solitude. She enjoys singing in the choir at church with her husband, as well as being a lector/reader at her church.

Made in United States
Orlando, FL
14 September 2025